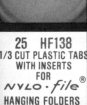

TYPOGRAPHY

⚡

LETTERING

⚡

BADGES

⚡

LOGOS

JUNK TYPE

BILL ROSE

UNIVERSE

To my wife, partner, and best friend, Teri.
Thank you for your encouragement, patience,
and unwavering support. I love you.

First published in the United States of America by
UNIVERSE PUBLISHING, a division of
Rizzoli International Publications, Inc.
300 Park Avenue South, New York, NY 10010
www.rizzoliusa.com

© 2017 Bill Rose
Introduction © 2017 Mike Essl

Designed by Kayleigh Jankowski

Printed in China

2022 2021 2020 / 10 9 8 7 6 5 4
Library of Congress Control Number: 2016918466
ISBN: 978-0-7893-3265-3

CONTENTS

FOREWORD
BY BILL ROSE

Junk Type was never meant to be a book. It started as nothing more than a few iPhone photos I had taken of some striking typography that caught my eye one day while junkin'—exploring the estate sales, antique stores, flea markets, garage sales, and architectural salvage yards I frequent on the weekends near my home in Minneapolis and whenever such places are nearby while traveling. Over the subsequent weeks, a small visual catalog of images started to take shape on my website, and before long this hobby turned into a full-blown obsession. I became fixated on documenting the seemingly endless stream of stunning letterforms I encountered. Suddenly, my quest to find vintage typography was the primary driver of these junk-filled expeditions. I always had one eye out for logos and badges and lettering styles that I'd never seen before. Ultimately the catalog grew into a stockpile of several hundred images that attracted a sizable following, a bit of media coverage, and the attention of my publisher. And now we're here. Who would have thought?

The images on these pages are the result of countless hours rummaging through vintage relics with excited anticipation about what I might find emblazoned on the front (or back, side, or bottom) of the next dusty artifact I dug up. Most of the designs featured here are no bigger than an inch or two wide. They are often so small that my lens had trouble focusing, given the close range of the subject and the poor lighting conditions of their surroundings.

The typography featured in this book was found adorning a broad spectrum of products, ranging from the dramatic and sometimes ornate packaging of consumer goods to the often more functional and utilitarian designs stamped onto industrial machinery. These styles, although greatly varied, are unified through the charming and character-rich aesthetic they share. All of these designs are from an era that predates computers and the specialized software used by modern-day graphic designers. Logos and letterforms were conceived, created, and produced manually on a drawing table using tools and techniques that are nearly obsolete today.

In an ironic but predictable twist, the distinct styles of these letterforms are inspiring a renaissance of vintage typography in contemporary design. Today's most influential graphic designers are producing type that borrows heavily from the designs of past generations. In fact, it's hard to go through a single day without seeing multiple instances of vintage-inspired typography, especially in advertising—billboards, storefront signage, television commercials—it's everywhere.

And while the spirit of this brand of typography is being kept alive in modern forms, in some ways this style is very much endangered. Products that used to come branded with machine-stamped chrome badges and hand-drawn typographical elements are now marked with plastic decals and vinyl stickers. The charming imperfections that resulted from registration errors on paper packaging have been nearly eliminated by technologies offering pixel-perfect precision. This is the new reality.

My hope is that *Junk Type* can serve as a reference guide, a resource that helps bridge the design and typographic styles of the past with those of today. Perhaps this book will even be a source of inspiration for whatever comes next.

BALDOR®
INDUSTRIAL MOTOR

THREE PHASE

CAT. NO.	CM3218T			
SPEC.	36B02Y46			
FRAME	184TC	SER.	F1180	
H.P.	5			
VOLTS	208-230/460			
AMPS	14.8-14/7			
R.P.M.	1725			
HZ	60	PH. **3**	CLASS	B
SER. F.	1.15	DES B	CODE	H
FULL LOAD EFF		%	P.F.	%
RATING				

CONNECTION

LOW VOLTAGE

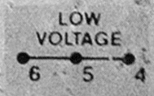

6   5   4

LINE

HIGH VOLTAGE

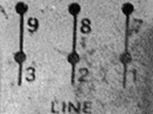

LINE

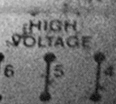

INTRODUCTION
BY MIKE ESSL

A few years ago I was at the Grand Canyon with my family. It was a beautiful day, my wife and son were looking out at the majestic view, and instead of joining them I was taking pictures of the 'Scenic View' sign nearby. The type was made in such a strange way and was hand-painted in bright yellow on a dark brown piece of wood. A router had been used to bore the type into the wood and that process had given the type its unique shape. I was still out by the car, taking photos of the sign, when I heard my wife say to one of the other sightseers, "Oh, he probably likes the type on the sign. He does that all the time."

Every graphic designer I know, myself included, has a collection of photographs of old type that we can't stop picking at. It's a disease we all share, though *Junk Type*'s author Bill Rose has a pretty serious case. If you look at my Instagram feed right now you see images of vinyl type peeling off the side of an ancient ice machine, rub-on transfer letters used on an emergency call box, and aged gold-leaf letters in the window of a local dry cleaner. Like most of us, I'm guilty of having nostalgia for an era when type was more visceral and made with materials like metal, wood, and plastic. Maybe working with type on a computer all day makes me crave letters I can touch, or that have been touched by time. But I know it's not just nostalgia that drives me to take these pictures: I also love to steal.

In my own work I steal to get unstuck. Working with letterforms can be tricky, but not so tricky that someone hasn't already figured it out. After all, there are only 26 letters you have to worry about at one time, and I bet that your unique combination of letters has not only been combined before, but probably in a more interesting way than what you're looking at on screen. Often I'll get stuck on one thing, like how an R is supposed to connect to other letters in a script typeface. If I'd had *Junk Type* at the time I could have turned to pages 22 and 23 and stolen ten different examples of lowercase-script Rs. Or occasionally I need to steal a certain style, like type made of metal, and *Junk Type* would have helped me there as well—pages 36 and 37 show type formed and stamped in metal. One of my favorite things is bending type to fit into a strange shape. I don't know of any book that teaches you the right or wrong way to do this, but the examples on pages 42 and 43 are a lot better than what I came up with. The electrifying examples found between pages 56 and 59 would have been perfect inspiration for a recent gig that required a word drawn with lightning.

Now I don't condone wholesale theft—don't just scan one of these logos, trace it, and call it a day. That would be tacky. Instead, lift one small moment, like the way the E is made of lightning bolts in the word 'Zipper,' or the way the word 'TRIFA' is stretched to fit into a shape. *Junk Type* is an archive of small ideas for you to lift and use in your work. And trust me, the artists that made the original work wouldn't mind if you lifted a few ideas. Back when this stuff was being made, they were stealing from each other all day long—leaning over their drafting boards and saying things like, "Maybe try the type the way we did that 'Frost-King' thing from last year." Between the 1920s and the 1950s, when most of this work was created using pencils, pens, brushes, and things like ruling and speedball pens, designers often worked in a bullpen with many other lettering artists. Jobs likely started and finished in a day. No fuss, no muss. Not only were they stealing from each other, they were encouraging it so they could knock off early.

Today, type design is everywhere, from the proliferation of advertising and signage in our streetscapes to the infinite wealth of language all over the Internet. There are more graphic design professionals working out there than ever before, and accessible software whose sole purpose is to make choices easier. If you're anything like me you're reading this introduction a few years after *Junk Type* made it into your library. Maybe you're sitting in front of the scanner or waiting for Adobe Illustrator to stop crashing. Your copy is probably littered with Post-It notes that remind you of what you stole and how it got you out of a jam. Remember all those gigs and all the design trends that came and went, and you'll see that the work shown here endures. I hope *Junk Type* helps you put more custom type into the world. I know it will help me.

14

GUARANTEED

TRADE

DUMACO

MARK

PRODUCTS

new...refreshing

GREENBRIER

MENTHOL MILD PIPE TOBACCO

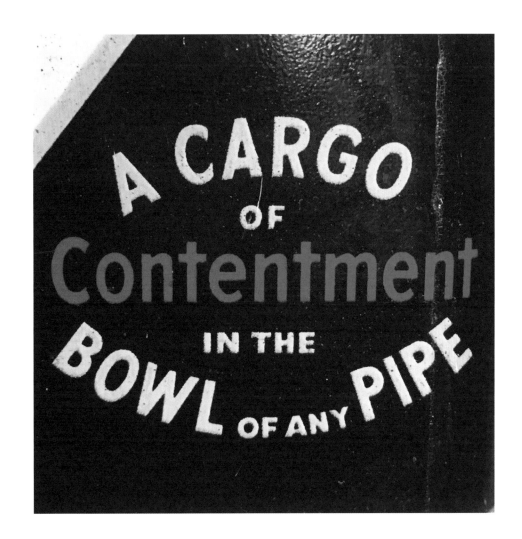

"Turner"
CEDAR RAPIDS IOWA

Beseler

"The New
Resco"
NAIL TRIMMER

Lady Hibbard

argus
preViewer
OR COLOR SLIDE

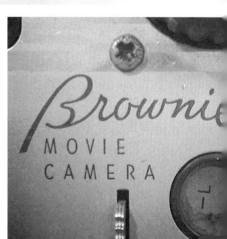

Brownie
MOVIE
CAMERA

Kuhlmann

National

Water Skis

Scripto
REG. U.S. PAT. OFF.
EXTRA STRONG

ST.

Elliotts

WHEARY
Stream Gard
PATENTED
STAINLESS STEEL TRIMMED
WHEARY TRUNK CO. RACINE, WIS.

HARVEY & HARRY
HUNTER'S

Honey

Ph: 262-2439
4125 E. Univ. Ave.
Des Moines, Ia. 50317
Ph: 262-7919
Runnells, Ia. 50237

NET WT.   OZ.
(6 LB.)

Medalist

500
GA.   2 9/16 IN.

Western
SUPER

-4 CH   S6140

Detmer

BINGO

The Square Deal Set

Mathematically Perfect

NO. 68

MANUFACTURED   BY

SELCHOW & RIGHTER CO.
NEW YORK, N.Y.

MADE IN U.S.A.

No. 9
REQUA'S
CHARCOAL

TRADE Ⓡ MARK

REG. US. PAT. OFF.

TABLETS

33

BARNETT & JAFFE

baja

MFRS. PHILA. PA. U.S.A.

Emdeko

CRAFTSMANSHIP

Starline

HARTMANN
TRIP-LEX
X - X - X
HARTMANN TRUNK CO.

Herkert & Meisel
TRUNK CO.
ST. LOUIS, MO.

Nu-Slant
by ALLIED

INSIST ON THIS BLUE SPOT

SEXAUER PATENTED

½"

BLUE SPOT BALLOON

TRADE MARK REG U S A PAT OFFICE

TANK BULB

WEBSTER·CHICAGO

WC

Recording Wire

W

Convenient
TABLES and
FORMULAS

HY-DUTY
BLOWER

SERIAL NO. 20810

SCHWITZER-CUMMINS CO.

INDIANAPOLIS U.S.A.

FARM·OYL

TRADE MARK REGISTERED

POST

Chew
Copenhagen

SUMMER
WINTER
SPRING
AND FALL

43

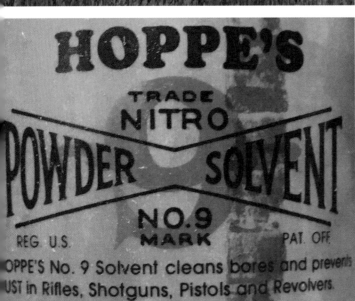

50

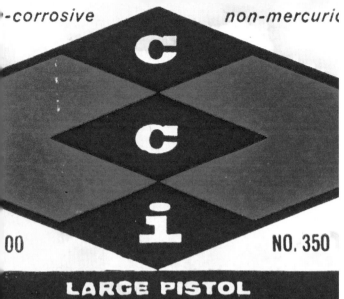

-corrosive   non-mercuric

C C i

00   NO. 350

LARGE PISTOL
PRIMERS

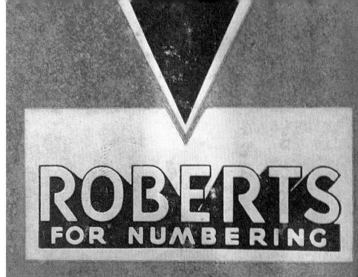

ROBERTS
FOR NUMBERING

CES
R

REDUC
FRICTIO

A
P
E
X

OP QUALITY

NEWALL

STATES ELECTRIC MFG

STATES

MINNEAPOLIS, MINN.

UNION   MADE

M 070058247

It's fun to make movies

with

Bell & Howell

8mm | CAMERAS
PROJECTORS
ACCESSORIES

54

"Easy-Lite" GOLD

HYTRON BALLAST TUBE

DIETZ ® STROBE
7-210 SN A0113

Electroized
ELECTROWELD·CHICAGO
RUSTPROOF

RADIO STROP DRESSING

Sterling

FIRE ENGINEER
INCINERATOR

MANUFACTURED BY
FIRE ENGINEERS INCORPORATED
HOPKINS, MINNESOTA
CORSICANA, TEXAS BOAZ, ALABAMA

Strong
ZIPPER
ESSANNAY ELE
1241 S. WABASH A

KEN·RAD
EPENDABLE
ADIO TUBE

PERFECTION
THRU RESEARCH

ELECTRONIC
TUBE

59

61

Hotpoint

THE
FRIEZ HUMIDISTAT
A PRODUCT OF
JULIEN P. FRIEZ & SONS, INC.
BALTIMORE   MARYLAND

*Livelyaire**

FAN

60 CYCLES · 115 VOLTS

*TRADE MARK

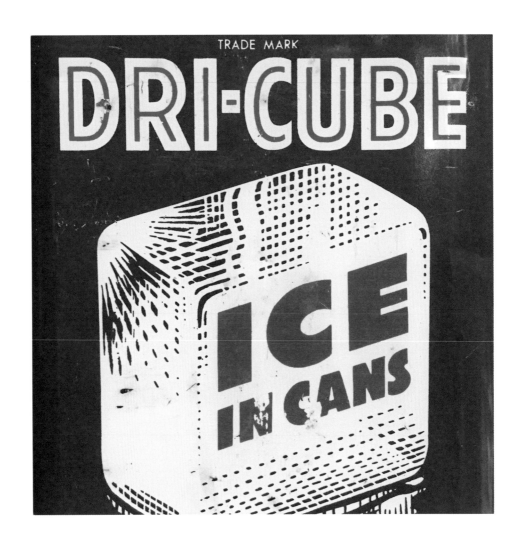

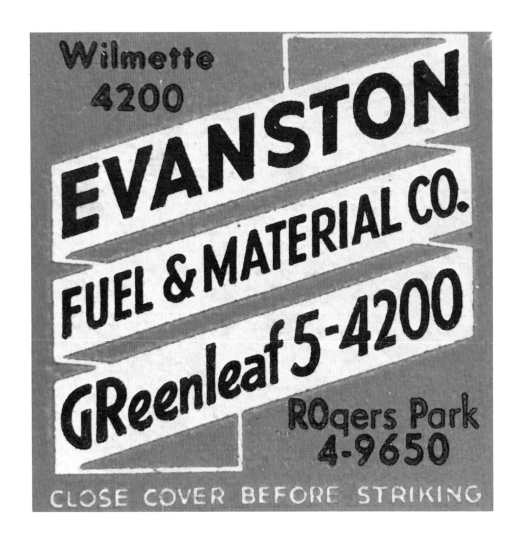

TM

DORMAN

'PRANG
WATER COLOR

OLD
FAITHFUL

CAST OPTICS
SUPER QUALITY
G·S FLEXO CRYST
REG U S PAT OFF
ROUND FLAT TO

LOOK FOR THE TRADE-MARK

TIMKEN ®

REGISTERED TRADE-MARK

ON EVERY BEARING YOU BUY

This bearing *Rolls* the Load

REGULATION
SEAL
JUSTRITE

The HOW AND WHY

Jointite
TRADE MARK
REG. U.S. PAT. OFF.
BOTTLE
CAPS

Victoreen

Marvel

MUELLER
Climatral

Edison

Surfmaster
WATER
SNOW

TYPE "F"

Peerless
MAGNARC
TRADE MARK REGISTERED

HIGH INTENSITY LAMP

SERIAL № | 25605

DIRECT CURRENT

| ARC VOLTS | 28-42 | ARC AMPS. | 32-75 |
| MOTOR VOLTS | 31-110 | MOTOR AMPS. | 0.5-1.4 |

U.S. PATENT NOS.

| 1634769 DATED 7-5-27 | 2097767 DATED 11-2-37 |
| 1665410 " 4-10-28 | 2115688 " 4-26-38 |

— MFD. BY —

J. E. McAULEY MFG. CO.
CHICAGO 6, ILL.
UNITED STATES OF AMERICA

Bachelors Friend
TRADE MARK

GUARANTEED SOX

Shelvador

Cinématic
UNIVERSAL CAMERA CORPORATION
NEW YORK N.Y. U.S.A.

MAIN ON   LAMP ON

Jackson Graves

NICOLLET MALL   SOUTHDALE
HIGHLAND   HAR-MAR
    BROOKDALE

Airequipt
MAGAZINE

Eklund
Clothing Co.
4th and E. HENN.
SINCE 1893

SHINOLA

REG. U.S. PAT. OFF.

DRESS PARADE

APPLICATOR
INSIDE

BUTLER BROTHERS
MAJESTY
NEEDLES

MADE IN ENGLAND

Acme
ADJUSTABLE
DRESS FORM
L & M ADJUSTABLE FORM CO.
BROOKLYN 21, N. Y.
SIZE
B

NICKEL 15¢ PLATED
MILWARDS
Needles ®
MADE IN ENGLAND

LARGE EYE NEEDLES

SINGER SEWING MACHINES

WINDOPAK

Sewing Needles

JOHN H. PRATT
GEO. P. FARMER

JOHN ENGLISH & CO.

NEW IMPROVED
EASY WAY
DARNER

WILL NOT SLIP OFF NEEDLE

DO YOUR DARNING THIS MODERN WAY

FITS ALL MAKES OF MACHINES

PRICE PER SET 50¢

Western Stationery Co.
Topeka, Kansas

EXTRA SPRING 25¢

12 STITCHES TO AN INCH

Domestic
ROTARY ELECTRIC
SEWING MACHINES
Series 153

Willcox & Gibbs
Sewing Machine Co.
658 BROADWAY
NEW YORK
12525

J. R. BAUMAN
NORMAL MODEL FORM
INC.
MODEL FORMS
FOR
DESIGNERS & FACTORIES
134 WEST 25TH ST.

Stella

ARMED - FRETTE - ARMIERT

GILTED - DORÉ - DOUBLÉ

THE MARK
OF
QUALITY

HOPPE'S ®

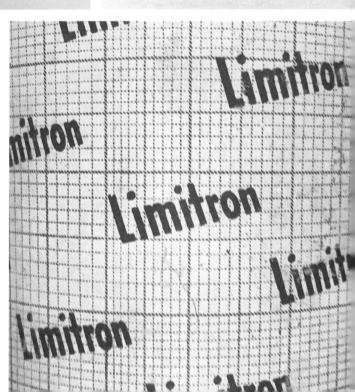

Chicago
MADE BY
AUTOMATIC PENCIL SHARPENER CO.
CHICAGO. U.S.A.

Camp's
Latex Concret
TRADE MARK

REPAIR • TOPPING • WELDING

For Smoothing or Patching Rough, Spalling, Trowel-Ma
Uneven or Broken Concrete and Masonry Surface

Eliminates
CHIPPING • ROUGHENING
PRIMING • CURING

Self-Bo

USE IND

coast to coast

THE CAMP COMPANY, INC.

codo

MANUFACTURING CORP.

**GENERAL OFFICE & FACTORY
LEETSDALE, PA. 15056**

NOT JUST A FUSE

Ordinary fuses cannot protect motor
against burnout—but Fustat fuses can—
they have a therma
cutout with
the fuse

BUSS
Fustat Fuse
Underwriters
Lab Inspected
S

MAZE NAILS

MAZE NAILS

GENUINE

TRADE-MARK.

HOLD FAST.

REGISTERED.

NAILS

CHAS. F. BAKER & CO

Boston, Mass., U.S.A.

Sole Manufacturers.

FAMILY BRAD AND NAIL ASSORTMENT

INSULATED STAPLES

Est. 1848

COBB C&D INC. DRI

PLYMOUTH, MASS.

MANUFACTURERS OF

FINE QUALITY

SOLID RIVETS

WASHERS — BURRS

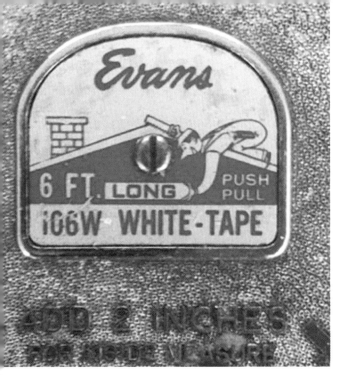

Evans

6 FT. LONG — PUSH PULL

i06W WHITE-TAPE

ADD 2 INCHES FOR INSIDE MEASURE

COBBLERS NAILS

BAKATAX

¼ LB NET

ATLAS

REG. U.S. PAT. OFF.

ATLAS

BRIGHT STEEL WIRE

BRADS

TOY WRINGER

ANCHOR BRAND

TRADE MARK.

LOVELL MFG. CO.

ERIE, PA.

ANCHOR
BRAND
CLOTHES
WRINGERS

BEST ON
EARTH
EVERY ONE
WARRANTE

MADE BY

STRATA-BOW.
MADE IN U.S.A.

VOYAGEUR

FAIRMONT

MINNEAPOLIS, MINN.

445

UNION MADE

ISSUED BY UNITED BROTHERHOOD OF CARPENTERS AND JOINERS OF AMERICA
ORGANIZED 1881 · REGISTERED 1900

THE Setwell
TRADE MARK WARRANTED
PAT. 1955792
SELF-OPENING - ROLLER BEARING
MADE IN U.S.A.

GLOBE-WERNICKE

ESQUIRE
SHOE VALET
De Luxe

PAT PEND

"WHERE YOU ALWAYS BUY THE BEST FOR LESS"

GIBSON'S
GIBSON'S
DISCOUNT CENTER

GENERAL DUTY
Vacu-Break ®
SAFETY SWITCH
Clampmatic ®
CONTACTS

CAT. NO. | JN-321

FIREBIRD

BY BURR-SOUTHERN

CITY OF INDUSTRY, CALIFORNIA

EAGLE

EAGLE
MIRADO
LEADS

MANUFACTURED BY
PELOUZE MANUFACTURING CO
CHICAGO, U.S.A.

Sioux
Mox

THE
HALL'S
SAFE CO
CINCINNATI
TRADE
MARK

NATIONAL TOURNAMENT
CHALK
TRADE   MARK REG
GOLDENROD

GOLDEN PARROT STRAIGHT PINS BRAND

BLUE JAY
REG US PAT OFF

PHONE 191
BIRD ISLAND DAIRY
BIRD ISLAND, MINN.
PASTEURIZED MILK

QUEEN
REVOLVING SEAT & SHELL BOX
MFD. BY
QUEEN STOVE WORKS INC. ALBERT LEA, MINN

Atlas

KLIX

TRADE MARK
FAIRBANKS
PRECISION
SCALES

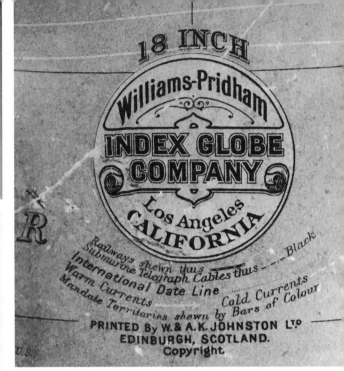

18 INCH
Williams-Pridham
INDEX GLOBE
COMPANY
Los Angeles
CALIFORNIA

Railways shewn thus ——————
Submarine Telegraph Cables thus ——— Black
International Date Line
Warm Currents
Mandate Territories shewn by Bars of Colour
Cold Currents

PRINTED BY W. & A.K. JOHNSTON LTD
EDINBURGH, SCOTLAND.
Copyright

R
U.S.

ATLAS MILLING CO.

ATLAS

1920
NEW WORLD
ATLAS

DIETZGEN

GLOBE

12077-18

MADE IN U.S.A

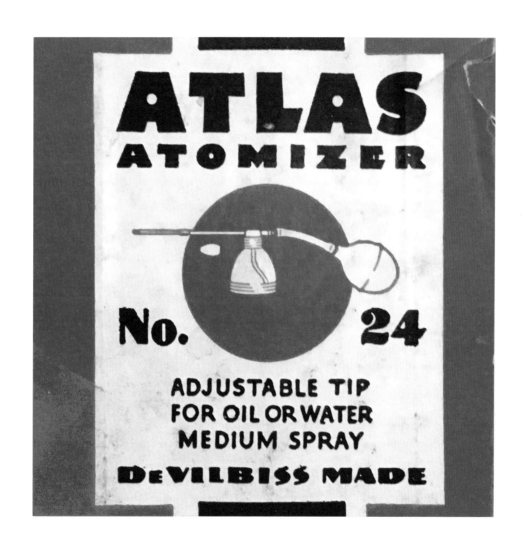

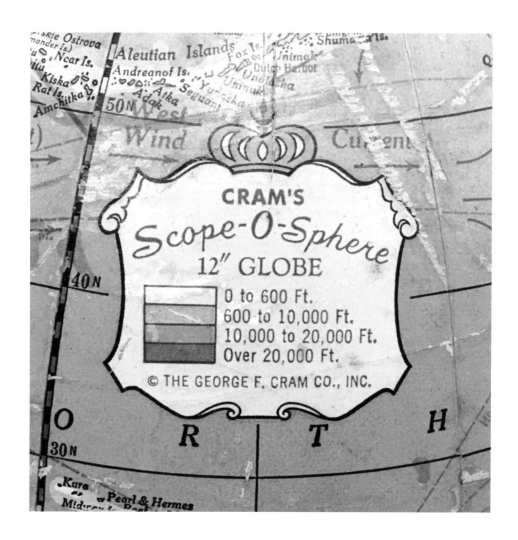

AMPEREX

Schmitt
MINNEAPOLIS

TRANSOGRAM
GOLD MEDAL
Toys
and
Games
Since 1915

...LIES WITH NATIONAL SAFETY STANDARDS · DESIGN
AMERICAN
GAS
ASSOCIATION
· CERTIFIED ·

MERIT
CTC
Since 1924
FINE
RADIO
PARTS

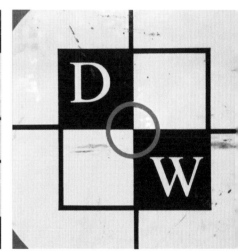

D
W

DU MONT

Red Cross
1 INCH
J&J
TRADE MARK
10 YARDS
Bandage

Logan

LIFE SAVER
Y
JONES & YANDELL DIV. ATCO.
CANTON, MISS.
MADE OI *Ensolite*

Standard Brand

ESNA

BRIGHT PLATED HARDWARE • CHEMICALLY TREATED AGAINST RUST AND CORROSION • DURABLE BAKED ENAMEL FINISH • CONTINUOUS PIANO HINGE • WATERTIGHT
Simonsen
CHICAGO 51, ILL.
STREAMLINE QUALITY
FORM FITTING HANDLES • PATENTED ADJUSTABLE DIVIDERS • RADIUS CORNERS THROUGHOUT • SEAMLESS DEEP DRAWN & FABRICATED BOXES

PHILCO
Famous for
QUALITY
the World Over

TEKTRONIX

DURO TEST

MARSCHALL

FILM
PAKO
SERVICES

ELECTRICITY
MAKES A WORLD
OF DIFFERENCE

CLAROSTAT

REG. U. S.   PAT. OFF

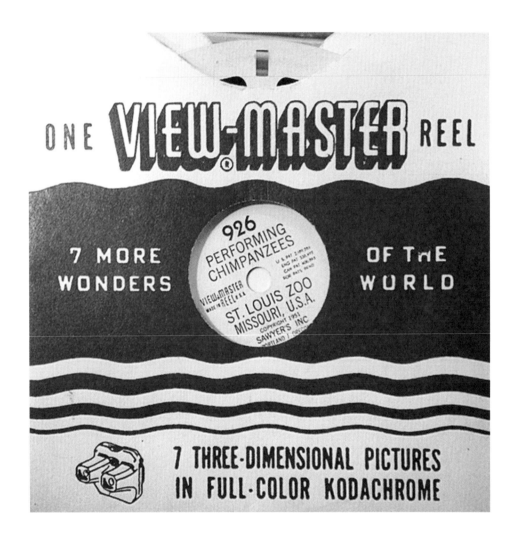

COMPTOMETER ®

FELT & TARRANT MANUFACTURING CO.

09 09 09

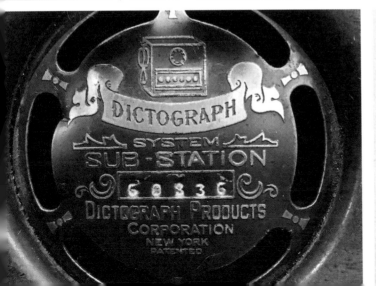

DICTOGRAPH
SYSTEM
SUB-STATION
68836
DICTOGRAPH PRODUCTS
CORPORATION
NEW YORK
PATENTED

25 HF138
1/3 CUT PLASTIC TAB
WITH INSERTS
FOR
NYLO·file ®
HANGING FOLDERS

The CHECKOMETER

CHECK-WRITER
AND
PROTECTOR

Made By
THE CHECKOMETER COMPANY
CHICAGO, ILL., U. S. A.

G 437604

The OLIVER
STANDARD VISIBLE WRITER·
No. 3.

REMINGTON
FACTORY GUARANTEED
Complete Audible Range Reproduction

ROLL OUT
Conserv-a-File
ME STEEL
CORP.
BROOKLYN, N.Y.
11232
H 407

ROYAL

Lettergraph
Model E
SER. NO.
E-9740
MADE IN
U.S.A.
PATS. APPD. FOR
HE HEYER CORPORATION · Chicago, Ill.

DURO

ART
SUPPLY CO.

A Subsidiary of Duro Decal Co Inc.

MINNESOTA PAINTS

MADE EXCLUSIVELY FOR Walgreen's MASTERCRAFT TOOL & TACKLE UTILITY BOX

Guaranteed Highest Quality
CRAFTSMAN
REGISTERED TRADE MARK

SPEEDBALL

Perfection

COLORING SET

pastoil
TRADE
MARK
Reg.

ARTISTS' OIL PASTELS

MADE IN JAPAN
DISTRIBUTED BY
PERMANENT PIGMENTS, INC.
CINCINNATI 12, OHIO

permanent pigments

EXCEPTIONALLY BRILLIANT • NON-DUSTING

16 Studio Size Sticks • No. 116

4 OZ. NET

VINCE

The Scientific Mouth-Wash

REG. U. S. PAT. OFF.

Combining the prophylactic and sterilizing qualities of true, high-test Sodium Perborate with aromatical agents, scientifically introduced, to make a palatable, refreshing and effective preparation for use in Oral Hygiene.

VINCE LABORATORIES, INC.
New York City
MADE IN U.S.A.

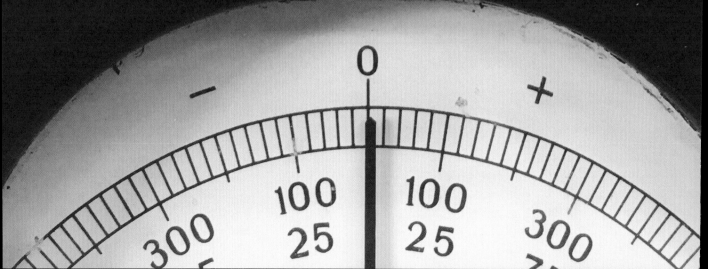

McCORMICK VENDING MACHINE COMPANY

GREENVILLE, N.C.

MANUFACTURERS AND DISTRIBUTORS

QUALITY COIN OPERATED
VENDING AND AMUSEMENT MACHINES
"EVERYTHING WORTHWHILE THAT OPERATES WITH A COIN"

SUPPLIES AND REPAIR PARTS FOR ALL
MAKES COIN CONTROLLED
MACHINES

PHONE, WIRE   OR WRITE

141

DUPONT PHOTO PRODUCTS

REG. U.S. PAT. OFF.

E. I. DUPONT DE NEMOURS & CO. (INC.)
PHOTO PRODUCTS DEPT.   WILMINGTON, DELAWARE

MRK 010
LINO-WRIT
DIRECT WRITING PAPER

IMPORTANT: OPEN ONLY IN SUBDUED LIGHTING

While this product will be replaced if defective in manufacturing, labeling or packaging, it is sold without express or implied warranty or liability of any other kind.

Made in U.S.A.   Printed in U.S.A.

STANDARD WEIGHT

SPEC. No.

12 x 200   2

0808   57010 2179 7-69   ORDER CODE

EMULSION NO.   REF. NO.   USE BEFORE   LW-5B MRK 010

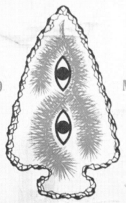

PREMISES PROTECTED

ARROWHEAD

SECURITY &
MAINTENANCE
PATROL

APPLETON
ELECTRIC COMPANY
CHICAGO, ILL.

FOOD
GUILD

GREEN LABEL

GRAYS

SINCE 1856

WOODLAND JUG

KEEPS HOT & COLD

FIBERGLAS INSULATED

POLORON PRODUCTS INC. NEW ROCHELLE N.

U.S. BERKEL

MODEL G

U.S. SLICING MACHINE CO.
LAPORTE, IND.

RADIO AND TELEVISION
TUBES

FUSETRON

Dual - Element
CLASS K9 FUSE

FRN 150
amp.

faLLine
ski wa
farts de sk

"Sunny Suzy"
WASHING
MACHINE

LEADER SPARKLERS

Union

TOP STAR

AMSCO

Boye
REG. U.S. PAT. OFF.

EAGLE

YECK Flexible

YANKEE GIRL

S.D.Co.

UNION MADE

SCRAP

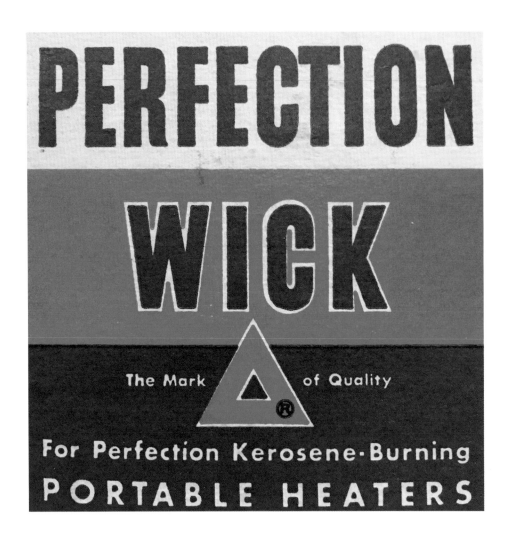

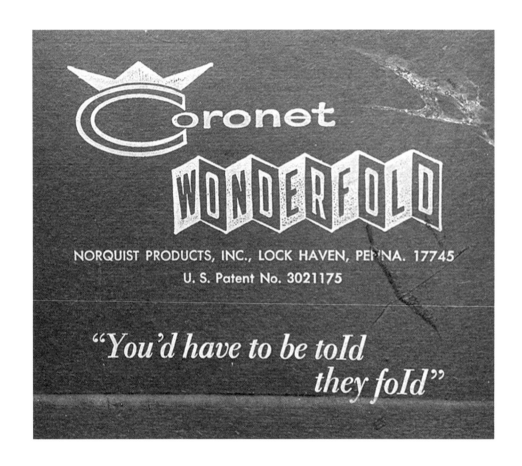

158

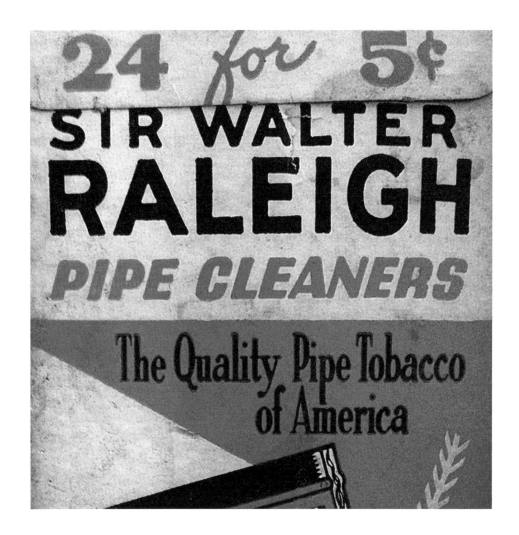

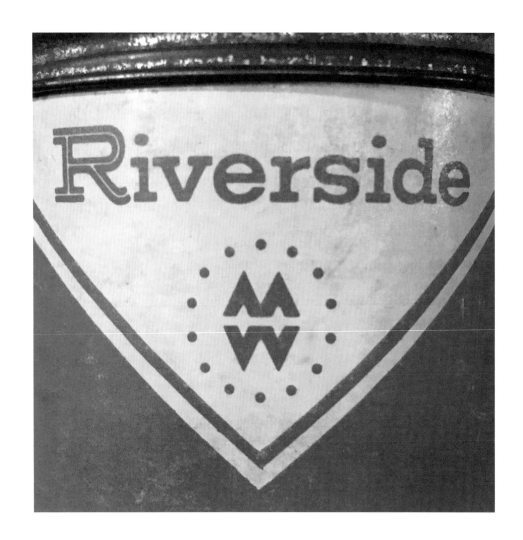

MOTOR
MONIZ
SIMONIZ®
PASTE FOR CARS
KEEPS COLORS
FROM FADING
3083
AND BEAUTIFIES ALL

Solvene

TYPEWRITER
CLEANER
®

Shedd's
FINE FOODS
¢

Schaller

National
NC
HRO "Sixty"

SELECTIVITY ▽

3 2 1

Silvertone
REG U S PAT OFF

Supertone
scale

Santiaga
CALIFORNIA
Melons

Simplex
TRADE MARK REG'D.
HEAVY
DUTY

Simpson
INSTRUMENTS THAT STAY ACCURATE

Compare... and you will

Buy

WELLS LAMONT

Gloves

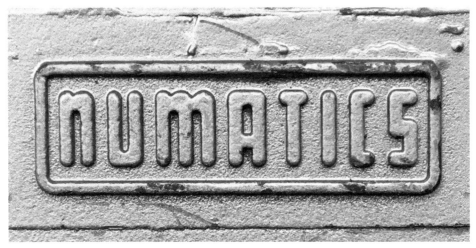

TUFBOY
REG. U.S. PAT. OFF.

SIX  FEET

NO. 306

179

Edgeworth

READY-RUBBED

EXTRA
HIGH GRADE

DEPENDABLE

United SINCE 1869 WIRE

BRAZING ALLOYS

PARA USO EXTERNO

IODUNTAL

LABS. HEMOL, SAN JUAN. P.R.

Thompson Products

THOMPSON PRODUCTS, INC.

CLEVELAND, OHIO, U.S.A.

SAGAMORE

STEEL PINS

PLATED

Intermatic

time-all
APPLIANCE TIMER

MODEL A221-4

SANFORD'S

<u>Pen</u>it

Violet

FOUNTAIN PEN INK

MADE IN U.S.A.

Norcor
Manufacturing Company, Inc.
GREEN BAY, WISCONSIN
SEATING THE WORLD
REG. U.S. PAT. OFF.

WesternField

CONSEW®

FOXBORO
REG. U.S. PAT. OFF.
Instruments
FOR
INDICATING
RECORDING
CONTROLLING

THREAD EZY
DARK
CUTTING
OIL
TB
TOLEDO-BEAVER Tools, Inc.
Toledo, Ohio, U.S.A.

Mitchell

T
TRINER
AIR MAIL
ACCURACY
SCALE

SEATER
HEATER
(TRADE MARK)

Flinch

REG. U.S. PATENT OFFICE

189

Cat. No. 3332

SNAPIT

SPEED-LOK

BELL OR CHIME

TRANSFORMER

115 VOLTS AC
50-60 CYCLES
16 VOLT OUTPUT

CABLE ELECTRIC PRODUCTS, INC., PROVIDENCE 7, R. I.